Nina Dont

the pirates we called

the pirates
we called

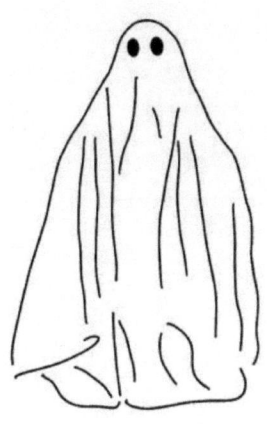

NINA DONT

Bibliografische Information der Deutschen Nationalbibliothek:
Die Deutsche Nationalbibliothek verzeichnet diese Publikation in der
Deutschen Nationalbibliografie; detaillierte bibliografische Daten sind im
Internet über http://dnb.dnb.de abrufbar.

Cover: Nina Dont

Herstellung und Verlag: BoD – Books on Demand, Norderstedt

ISBN: 9783757814380

Dear reader,
Thank you for picking up my words, it means a lot to me.
I'm not a poet but I needed to get some things off my chest
and even if it may not make sense sometimes, it was
therapeutic for me.
I'm excited to see where this prose poetry journey takes
me as an author and I hope you are too.
Thank you for leaving a kind review.

Acquaintance

[noun]

ac · quain · tance

a person whom one knows but who is not a particularly good friend

I am enraged

it's a burden
being this sad

when i really needed someone
you texted me
but when i poured my heart out
you left me on read
and it's been that way
ever since

Read

out of sight
out of mind
i guess
but at least you left me
with a million knives in my back

i was drawn to the attention
you granted me
but that doesn't make you a good
f
  r
    i
      e
        n
          d

and maybe
i was just a
charity project
until he gave you
a better one

you disguise your
words of terror
as words of truth
but
being honest
is different
from being hurtful
on purpose

it took me a long time
but
eventually
i realized
you couldn't care less
about the things
that are so important
to   m e

our late night
phone calls
made me feel important
until i found out
no one else was
available

& maybe you're ghosting me
because i'm a constant reminder
of what a shitty friend
you are

i knew it was over
when i watched your plant in my kitchen change
    from green
    to brown
    to death
    into the trash

along with our friendship

money isn't everything
say the ones
who used you for it

you say it was a misunderstanding

i think it was calculated

interesting
how we can talk for hours
about your problems
but the minute
i try to talk about mine
you suddenly have no time

the best times of my life
i had with you
but you can ghost me
only so many times
before even *i*
give up

it's the lack of closure
that's keeping me awake
a million things
that haunt me in the middle of the night

everything you do
is intentionally decisive
but i think it is delusional
and deceiving

calculated
you came for my throne
threw out my guards
packed up my silver
and came running to my woods
when they did the same to you

you broke me

so now
to protect myself
i only look for the worst
in every new person i meet

i watched you
ignoring me
breaking up our friendship
trying to get a clean slate
trying to shut me out
now i watch you
bringing me flowers and
mourning my grave

Casual

[adjective]

ca · su · al

met with on occasion
and known superficially

I am disappointed

it still hurts
and i'm still grieving

i remember screaming at you
silently
to want the same thing i did
   to be best friends
      to be more
         to be at least something
but then i remembered
i can't force a friendship

absurd
how you treated me
after i stopped giving you
what you thought
you deserved

you took advantage
of the fact
that i wanted
the friendship more than you did

in hindsight
in a way
we had a strange relationship

i considered you family
while you only called
when you needed
something

so many years we have shared
i confided in you
but
we grew apart
and that happens
but while i cared for you fondly
from a distance
i have learned
that you didn't even care enough
to call or text
after your heard my news

how could you forget the way you treated me?
while i'm the one
remembering every single
sleepless night
in the dark void of
our friendship

should i've noticed it sooner?
the way your eyes went empty
after i begged you
to stop taking
advantage of me

i gave you
  my time
    my youth
      my truth

and in return i got
  left out
    forgotten
      lost

i know i'm different when i'm with you
i'm defensive
i'm moody
i'm sad
but i'm too scared to be alone
to leave this toxic friendship

you say they are
words of honesty
i say they are
words of cruelty
and still
somehow
i'm convinced it was my fault

i introduced you two

and then

i lost both of you

i try to keep to myself
i rarely stand up for the things i believe in

but when i do
i lose entire friendships in the process

- how is that fair?

feeling like a burden
i open my mouth
try to let it all out
but where once was air
now everything is in despair
silent screams
that never leave my mouth
trying to remember
how it all went south

i always thought
it would be easy
letting go of someone
who wasn't yours
in the first place

it broke me
not the fact that
you did walk away
but how it seemed so easy for you
you left me
when i needed you the most

my phone is silent
like it's been for weeks now
i delete your number
and your messages
knowing
our memories
will haunt me forever

how do i get over a friendship
that just faded out?
no fights and
no responses to texts
no picking up the phone
and i'm left
confused
how it reached this point

once in a while

you just have to hit the breaks

when the friendship becomes too draining

and that's okay

even if it hurts

even if it wrecks you

even if you think you will never recover

at first it seemed

s

   p

      a

         c

            e

would be good for us

but little did we know

s

   p

      a

         c

            e

was the only thing

that worked for us

sometimes
it's the people you never would've guessed
who can actually hurt you the most

i'm still mourning
the fact that
giving us up
was the only thing
left to do

devastating realization
that in the end
i wasn't able to fix us

isn't it tragic
how we sometimes
only get to know people really well
at their eulogy?

Close

[adjective]

1 as in tight

having little space between items or parts

2 as in near

not being distant in time, space, or significance

I am thankful

it took me a long time
to realize
that the people i searched for my whole life
have been right in front of me

sometimes
you find your ride or dies
in the people you never would've guessed

the thing i love most about you
is that you're also
friends with my parents

the more time we spent together
the more i fall in love again
with life
with the endless possibilities of just being and with the
realization that you can do anything
with the right people in your corner

you are the reason
i believe in friendship again
eating dinner in full silence
and yet i'm convinced
it was the best talk i've ever had

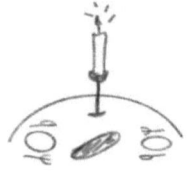

even when darkness surrounded us
we kept walking
into our shining future
we stayed being friends
against all odds
. glad i woke up just in time

my castle had crumbled
my kingdom ceased to exist
in the midst of my broken spirit
i was ready to give up
but when you entered my world
with the brightest colors
a mind full of stars and the wildest ideas
you brought everything back to life

you stared right into my imperfect soul
and decided to love me anyway

Intimate

in · ti · mate

[adjective]
1 as in close
intimate friends who can practically finish each other's
sentences

[noun]
1 as in friend
a person who has a strong liking for and trust in another

sometimes
things evolve

& still fall apart

it is no secret
that sometimes
lovers
started out as friends
but the higher you fly
the harder you fall

you read my poem

you say you love it

you ask me who it's about

y o u

we tried to deny it
i tried so hard to fight it
while she felt so secure
i still wasn't sure
i never dared to risk it
a spark so grand i couldn't miss it
we were close – she was my sister
still i regret i didn't kiss her

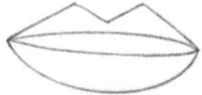

i worshipped
the ground you walked on
hoped and prayed
you weren't leading me on

i will always be there for you

don't say that

why?

because everyone who promised me that
left

i feel miserable
asking for you to hang out
two months in advance
while i see you on the internet
hanging out with them
everyday

pinky swears
were not made
to be broken

at least that's what i thought

It's always in the middle of the night when I lay awake and ask myself the same old questions. How did we go from daily talks to checking in every other week? How did we go from seeing each other every day to maybe once a month? Why didn't I realize you were going to slip out of my hands? Why wasn't I able to keep us from falling apart? Why did it shatter me into pieces?

deep black water below me
my eyes locked on the lighthouse of your island
i'm waiting for your guidance
to save me
to pull me out of this blackness
that is my heart
but you keep staring at me
you don't move
as i'm slowly sinking
water fills my lungs
and with my last breath
i whisper your name
until i drown
in my own sea of tears

you seem merry
in those pictures
but every smile breaks my heart
because i remember
once
i was your counterpart

i had an umbrella
big enough for the both of us
but you decided to follow the people
  who
  left
  you
standing in the rain in the first place

writing pages about our broken friendship
thinking about everything
i could've done differently
and there you are: living, thriving
as if nothing ever happened
but i'm still here
where you left me
still trapped in my thoughts and memories
i never moved on

once
we were beautiful
we whispered secrets to each other
holding hands in crowded rooms
gazing into each other's eyes
knowing exactly what was on our minds
because yes
we were once beautiful

by the time you brought me gerbera flowers
our story was already over
i had waited a long time
on your gingko tree to cut through
the blackberries
inside of me
because
the violets had vanished
and all that's left is the
linden tree creeping out of the
black hole that once was my
h e a r t

- say it in the language of flowers

did it shatter me, how you could leave me so easily
while i considered you my family?

yes.

we were acquaintances
became friends
and then family
silly me
i thought we would be this close forever
i never thought there would be a time
we would be strangers again

Ending
en · ding
[noun]

conclusion
the last part of a process or action

and yet ...
i still got hope

we were the queens
a whole kingdom to ourselves
like pirates we crossed
stormy seas and conquered new land
as artists we painted our future together
but just like icarus
we flew too high
got burned
and watched everything turn to ashes

i'm fine
except for the times i'm not
i'm fine
i say to make them happy
i'm fine
i say barely holding on
i'm fine
but i'm in pieces

they say
the ghosts of your past
help you understand your future

but what if …
we called the pirates instead?

what if …
instead of helping us
they kidnapped us and held us for ransom

what if …
instead of fighting them
we let them break us
and finally
we joined them

i grew fond of my past mistakes
visiting me
it's the only time
i don't feel lonely

it's unbearable
for me to accept
that some people
only stay in your life
for a limited amount of time
moving on is the hardest part

i often daydream about
my heart getting fixed by you
my broken trust
being repaired
and my soul finally at peace

i dreamt about my future for so long
i saw milestones
triumphs
and a lot of adventures
but no matter what i pictured my future to look like
i always saw myself with you

i hope you remember me
and all the good times we shared
i hope you tell everyone about us and
i hope when you look at our pictures
they warm your heart
i hope that when you talk about us
you remember to tell the funny stories
i hope you remember me and when you do
just know
my door will always be open

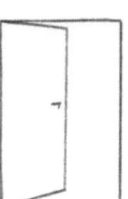

one day
i'm sure
we'll be fine again

The End

Part I

Thanks to ...

... Laura, Simone and Kimberly for being such great and supportive friends and for proofreading this book.

... my mom for being my biggest supporter.

... Jenni, Alice and Julia for being the brightest lights in my darkest times.

... April for being a great friend and colleague and for sharing all your knowledge.

... you for giving my words a chance.

About the author

Nina Dont lives with her family near Frankfurt in Germany. She writes novels and short stories and sometimes even poetry.
Contact her via E-Mail (ninadont@gmx.de) or Instagram (@ninasbooktalk) or check out her website (www.ninadont.de) for further information.

Definitions
https://www.merriam-webster.com/

Nina Dont